# The DIY Geodesic Growdome

## by simonthescribe

ISBN: 978-1-326-53681-7

Photography and images by Simon Mitchell

Produced at simonthescribe

simonthescribe.co.uk

# CONTENTS

# Introduction

Mostly I just love food. It amazes me when I go to a shop and see the prices – how can people produce food so cheaply? If you have ever tried to grow your own food you know it takes a lot of work to germinate the seeds, nurture the young plants with warmth, water and light and then grow them on in a sometimes inhospitable environment full of slugs and snails and inclement and unpredictable weather.

Economies of scale is one answer to the above question and the food you see in shops is mass produced, mostly with the aid of chemicals, and grown on soil which has had its mineral content so depleted that the resulting food is virtually nutritionally useless.

For someone who wants whole food and enjoys the contact with nature that this gives, a growing greenhouse is essential given the weather in the UK. So this little book charts my journey into making my own perfect greenhouse / growdome – a two-frequency, hemispherical icosahedron – with full instructions on how to make one for yourself.

Please let me know how you get on with your own greenhouse or growdome – you can email me at: simon@makeagreenhouse.co.uk

simonthescribe

# 1. What is a greenhouse?

At its most basic a greenhouse is any structure that can protect and nurture your plants to maximise their growth. This can be as simple as a bit of cling film over a pot to the glorious structures of Kew Gardens or the Eden Project.

There are many ways to grow food in your own home and garden - even if it is tiny. Yes, it is way more time consuming than popping down the shops to buy mass-produced vegetables that have systematically had all their minerals and amino acids removed by processing techniques, but it holds its own reward. When you become involved in the life of plants or animals, it opens a window in the universe.

To start with, and to get you thinking about greenhouses, here are a few ways to get yourself some protected food growing spaces:

## 1. Sprouting seeds

Anyone can grow sprouting seeds such as radish, alfalfa, mung beans, lentils, quinoa, wheat, aduki beans or chick peas. It is a great way to find out whether or not you can enjoy growing your own food. Mixed packs of seeds are readily available from health food shops, as are small stacker trays for home growing. They can be grown easily in a jar with a draining top.

Sprouted seeds contain a powerhouse of nutrients with high concentrations of essential enzymes, proteins, minerals, trace elements and natural vitamins. They also have an excellent fibrous value that helps to regulate the digestion and is kind to the intestines. Because they grow right up to the moment they are harvested there are very few nutrients lost - more fresh food straight from the kitchen. Sprouted seeds are delicious in sandwiches, salads, stir fries, soups, stews and dips. My personal favourites are sprouted Fenugreek seeds, a sublime taste!

## 2. Bottle Garden

A bottle garden is a step-on from seed sprouting. It is another set-up for an internal windowsill but it can work just as well outside if the weather is mild enough for growing. Make sure the plants get a mix of sun and shade, also air, as they are very sensitive to heat and moisture levels and can rot or wilt easily. I have harvested small lettuces and rocket in mid-winter using recycled two-litre water bottles on my kitchen windowsill, but to be fair, it wasn't a huge crop.

To make a mini windowsill greenhouse by re-purposing a plastic bottle, cut three-quarters of the way round the bottle about 4 inches up from the base. Make some drainage holes in the bottom and put in a layer of gravel and some seed compost. You can also use this process to bring-on seeds early for planting out.

Figure 1: Simple growing methods

## 3. Window Box

If there isn't a drainage system built into your window box, make sure it has holes and that the leakage isn't going to damage anything in the building by leaking into the sill. Put down a layer of pebbles or small stones to aid water dispersal, otherwise your box will be prone to rot and mould. For best results use a 50/50 mix of loam and coir compost without added insecticide. Fill to two-thirds with compost.

Put in seeds, or transplant your seedlings or plants to the box and top up with compost, leaving about an inch for watering. Give them plenty of growing room, about three herbs or lettuces to a two-foot long box. Keep it watered and pest/weather free and you should be cropping within two or three months. This is great for small, early salad greens and kitchen herbs.

## 4. Pots

Pots outside in the garden or on the patio give you a controlled growing environment. Even the smallest garden can accommodate a few pots of herbs. The key is to create the right conditions for each plant you decide to grow. Do they prefer sun or shade? Do they like it damp or dry, hot or cool? Part of the joy of growing is finding out how to position and nurture each plant.

There are many cheap import pots available from garden centres now and pots can be used indoors as well as outdoors. They are suitable for small patios, balconies and safe rooftop locations although they are likely to need constant watering in the summer on a roof. Automated watering systems are pretty easy to make though and solar power is ideal to power the pump as when the sun shines they need watering the most. You can even drip feed using water pressure from a well-positioned water butt. It is a good idea to raise garden pots from the ground a little to allow for proper drainage.

I found a half-dozen ceramic, chimney-lining tubes in the garden and these make great pots – as would drainage tubes. Simply place them upright in-situ in the garden. You can make sure they drain by dropping some gravel or non-toxic waste-material to allow space for water to collect on the way out, then fill them up with your preferred growing medium. I put seeds right in the top of these, water them in and then seal the top off with a small piece of polytunnel liner, cut to size. This creates a perfect little greenhouse to grow the seed where you want it and can offer some protection from slugs and snails as they germinate.

Figure 2: Simple growing methods 2

## 5. Roof top box

If you want to go a bit larger than pots, its quite simple to make (cat proof) mini-gardens from single sheets of 8 x 4 foot marine ply. I used mine on a flat roof but you can site them anywhere suitable.

I inset the base to allow it to dry out underneath and jigsawed the base with notches to improve aeration and drill holes to allow water drainage. I also made the back a little higher to install mirror tiles and improve the light for plants at the front. Although this will weigh quite heavy when it has about 10 inches of soil in the bottom I am also fixing it with batons to the outside wall to make it wind-proof for safety – I live in Cornwall and things can get quite 'exposed' here occasionally.

I also covered this rooftop box with chicken wire to stop domestic cats using it as a toilet. In early spring I also put on a layer of polythene over the seeds to bring them on. I used this one to successfully to grow a selection of early spring greens.

## 6. Raised beds

I have experimented with several ways of making these, mostly from rocks which seem to make-up a large part of my garden on the edge of Bodmin Moor. Another raised bed was made from a large slab of concrete two-feet out from a wall, with the ends made from old blocks. A third technique was to use sticks and carpet to hold enough soil to raise-up a bed. Raised beds are most useful as they allow some protection from crawly things that eat your food and you don't have to bens so far down to service of harvest the plants. But most of all, it is easy to add hoops to the top and layer over some poly tunnel liner or recycled plastic sheeting to make a small greenhouse to give your plants a head start.

Rock raised bed

Tyre raised bed

Stick and carpet bed

Home-made greenhouse

Figure 3: Simple growing methods 3

## 7. Tyre stacks

OK so many of you will find this technique of making a raised bed visually undesirable, but it is particularly effective and a great bit of repurposing.

Shown in Fig. 3 is a photo of potatoes growing in tyre stacks. This technique works well and gives a controlled growing environment for squash, courgettes, broad beans, I've even grown some whopping marrows in them. The tyre walls absorb the rays of the sun and warm up the soil, which helps stimulate the roots of the plant. The inside of the tyres hold water pockets so that the roots can drink from each tyre. Try not to leave gaps for slugs and snails to live in the tyres too!

With some potato varieties you can build-up the soil and tyres and layer the side-shoots into the soil to become roots, increasing your crop size dramatically. Watering, feeding, tending the plants and harvesting are all made easier with the elevation. It is also a good way of breaking-in new ground in as it suppresses the weeds in the soil under the tyres.

As an update to this technique: Although this is a great bit of recycling and a useful way of using land, there is increasing evidence though, that the tyres may well be leaching toxins into the soil and plants that grow there. I have stopped using tyres for this and now use a three-foot diameter, cylindrical, metal-mesh frame, lined with chicken wire. As the potatoes grow, fill the cylinder with soil and stop it falling out with a layer of straw. Layer the side-shoots down into the soil to root and grow potatoes.

## 8. Vertical gardening

This has become all the rage in cities, but to an extent people have always grown things up screens at least. Vertical wall gardening has now become an architectural feature in the greening of urban spaces.

'Le Mur Vegetal' first coined by Patrick Blanc can be seen all over. Specially designed (and expensive) architectural modules exist to suspend, water and feed plants grown vertically for effect.

But vegetable walls exist on practical as well as aesthetic levels. One such example is shown here in the photograph of Suzanne Forsling's Gutter Garden, which is a simply brilliant way to grow food that needs relatively little root space. The water supply is easily regulated using a drip feed and 'food' for the plants can be added to the water to supplement their restricted roots.

**Figure 4: A gutter garden**

## 9. Cold Frame

To be fair this is almost identical to the rooftop box above, but with a lid and used more traditionally to put pots under the protection of glass in the springtime and give them a head start. One tip I found in a growers book from 1911 included using an overnight candle underneath a raised, upside-down, ceramic flowerpot to heat the cold frame on frosty nights.

## 10. Covered shelf frame

These can be purchased quite cheaply or are easily made from pre-existing or built shelves. At their most basic you simply cover a shelved area with a polythene sheet to allow light through and trap the heat. They are often used in the UK for bringing on seedlings or for a source of fresh tomatoes, peppers, cucumbers or other garden delights.

I had intended to list many more types of greenhouse but, looking online, the range is so creative and imaginative it beggars belief. Just go online and put 'make a greenhouse' / images into a popular search engine to see for yourself. Wherever you live, whatever space you have, pretty much everyone should be able to grow some sort of food at home.

# 2. Why make a greenhouse?

**Figure 5: A newly installed, off-the-shelf greenhouse**

Having a greenhouse gives you a great advantage over the random elements of weather and climate. A small 'glasshouse' greenhouse can be purchased for a few hundred pounds but may well take a couple of days to put up, especially if you are putting in footings.

My personal preference is for making things and if this suits you – making your own greenhouse is a practical project that can save you considerable amounts of money. It takes about the same amount of time to put up a simple home-made greenhouse as it does an 'off the shelf' purchased variety.

There are many types of pre-made or kit-form greenhouses and domes available on the open market and you might choose one of these for ease. The most recent dome greenhouse I made worked out at one tenth of the cost of its purchased counterpart online. It may not be quite as beautiful but it is just as practical and I fully expect a five-year life at least from it. In its first winter season of gale-force winds in Cornwall – it is showing no sign of damage – but I have put it in quite a protected area.

**Figure 6: My latest home-made growdome**

The minimum requirements are that your greenhouse, whatever sort you choose, is sited with access to decent quality daylight, preferably with one long side (in the UK) facing south to maximise the light. You will also need sources of good quality soil and water. If you can set-up your greenhouse to capture and store the water that falls on it – that is going to save you energy and money. You can also use a black water-butt inside your greenhouse as a passive solar heat store to help keep your plants warm late into the evenings of sunny days. Some people are even putting closed composting systems into their greenhouse to capitalize on the heat they give out.

An unheated greenhouse can extend your growing season by a couple of months at least and adding heat means you may be able to grow all year round. You can protect your seedlings from the perversities of weather, wild and domestic animals and birds, even small people with footballs. Pretty much all of your plants can get a head start.

Last year – using a home made greenhouse – I extended my strawberry growing season from the two weeks around Wimbledon Tennis Championships, to a full eight weeks of regular cropping.

After choosing a suitable site for your greenhouse and checking the planning regulations for your area, think about what shape might fit there and what foundations it may need. The greenhouse shown at the start of this chapter, for example, was to be sited on a slope that meant level foundations had to be put in for blocks, which raised it up slightly at one end and gave more growing room. Also think carefully about water flow inside the greenhouse – where is the excess going to go? You might want to hose it down after washing the inside so should allow a good-size drainage hole somewhere in the base, where the natural run-off occurs.

It may be that several small, protected growing areas would suit you more than a single greenhouse. There are certainly reasonably priced seasonal hothouses on the market for tomatoes or seed propagation. You might want to make one on a wooden frame or create a polytunnel, you might wish to re-purpose some old windows or even create an underground greenhouse. My decision though was to use geodesics for a basic structure as I had always been fascinated by this form originated for building by Buckminster Fuller.

# 3. Introduction to Buckminster Fuller

*"You never change things by fighting the existing reality. To change something, build a new model that makes the existing model obsolete."*

You might want to skip this bit if you don't care where domes 'come from'. Me, I'm a bit nerdy and like to credit my teachers.

**Figure 7: Buckminster Fuller**

Buckminster Fuller was born on 12th July 1895 and lived for 88 years. Some people claim him to be one of the greatest thinkers of the 20th Century. At art college I even read one of his books called ***Critical Path***. It wasn't an easy read, but nestling there in the middle was a secret that changed my life. It was what Buckminster Fuller called the 'Law of Precession' and it was based on some of his observations, the results of which he lived his life by also. But I'm getting ahead of myself here - we'll come to 'Precession' in a few minutes.

Times were pretty harsh in the early 1900's and Buckminster Fuller lost a daughter to illness in circumstances that caused him to feel pretty bad about himself. According to history he was so unhappy he was even considering taking his own life. But a voice popped into his head and said: "your life is not yours to take."

Now this stopped him dead in his tracks and resulted in him asking himself who owned his life, then possibly THE QUESTION: "What then, is the purpose of my life?"

To cut a long story short, he answered the question for himself and resolved from that stage on to design and make things to solve global problems surrounding housing, shelter, transportation, education, energy, ecological destruction, and poverty, which he did successfully for the rest of his life.

> ***"I set about fifty-five years ago to see what a penniless, unknown human individual with a dependent wife and newborn child might be able to do effectively on behalf of all humanity..."***

These are just some of his inventions:

### Dymaxion car

In 1933 he presented his plans for the three-wheeled Dymaxion Car with rear steering and front-wheel drive powered by a Ford engine. The aerodynamic shape, most closely related to high performance yachts, came partly from Fuller's co-designer, the shipbuilder Starling Burgess. Unfortunately the rave reviews of the car's styling, speed and maneuverability were tragically undermined when the first of three prototypes was rammed and overturned, killing the driver, outside the entrance to the 1933 Chicago World's Fair.

### Dymaxion house

In 1940, in anticipation of the bombing of British cities, he was asked by the British War Relief Organization to design an emergency shelter. Fuller worked with a grain silo manufacture, using curved galvanised steel to develop a self-supporting structure in a circular shape. The unit was designed to be set up and taken down easily. Metal for its construction was, however, never made available by the British Government as it was needed for the production of armaments. When the US entered World War II, Fuller's units were commissioned as emergency accommodation for the air force.

The development of this was called a Dymaxion House. Made from lightweight steel, duraluminium and plastic and suspended from a central mast from which the rooms radiated in a hexagonal plan, the Dymaxion House was conceived not as private property, but rather as temporary, transportable space that could be rented – rather like a telephone issued by a telephone company.

**Figure 8: Fuller's Dymaxion car and Dymaxion house**

## Fuller Projection Map

Also know as the "Dymaxion Map," this is the only flat map of the entire surface of the Earth which reveals our planet as one island in one ocean, without any visually obvious distortion of the relative shapes and sizes of the land areas, and without splitting any continents. It was developed by R. Buckminster Fuller who "By 1954, after working on the map for several decades," finally realized a "satisfactory deck plan of the six and one half sextillion tons Spaceship Earth."

The Dymaxion World Map was his attempt to resolve the problem of how best to represent a spherical world on a flat surface, with true scale, true direction and correct configuration. In orthodox cartography to present one of these attributes accurately others must be distorted but The Dymaxion World Map's distortions are distributed proportionally within each of its fourteen segments.

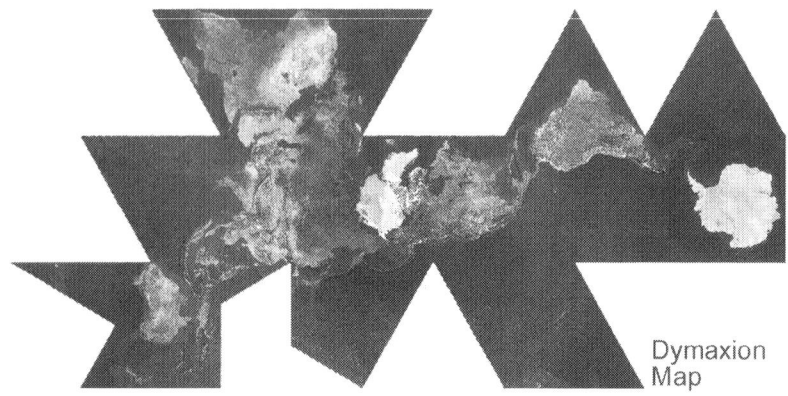

Dymaxion Map

**Figure 9: Fuller's Dymaxion world map**

This map, unlike the ones we are used to, shows all the countries of the earth joined, as one. This was very much part of Fuller's philosophy. Fuller also repeatedly makes it very clear that the scarcity paradigm that so many economists espouse is a thing of the past. This way of viewing the world no longer accurately describes the world.

The past 100 years of history show that man has been able to consistently and constantly do more with less. The human ability to invent and use technology has made the world abundant. The problem lies not in mans' ingenuity and inventiveness but in mans' greed. For man constantly makes the world scarce through war and greed. That is why so many people starve and suffer.

This makes a lot of sense to me. We only lose our energy in fighting 'the system out there' and we will never change it much. And we all know its days are numbered. Much better is to spend our time making new systems that work for us and people like us. If they work – other people will adopt them.

Fuller believed in having the courage to stand up for truth rather than simply following the course of least resistance. He calls people to unite and transcend to change the world around us. Since the ability to transform our world is in our hands, we have a tremendous responsibility to shape the world for the benefit of humanity and the good of others.

*"Whether it is to be Utopia or Oblivion will be a touch-and-go relay race right up to the final moment. . . Humanity is in 'final exam' as to whether or not it qualifies for continuance in Universe"*

He then invented a 'game' about this very thing.

## The World Game

Buckminster Fuller was convinced that we could achieve a higher standard of living without anyone profiting at the expense of another so that everybody can enjoy the whole earth.

World Game, sometimes called the World Peace Game, is an educational simulation developed by in 1961 to help create solutions to overpopulation and the uneven distribution of global resources. This alternative to war games uses Fuller's Dymaxion Map and requires a group of players to cooperatively solve a set of metaphorical scenarios, thus challenging the dominant nation-state perspective with a more wholistic "total world" view. The World Game that Fuller envisioned was to be a place where individuals or teams of people came and competed, or cooperated, to:

In 2001, a for-profit educational company named o.s. Earth, Inc. purchased the principal assets of the World Game Institute and has been offering a Global Simulation Workshop that is a 'direct descendant of Buckminster Fuller's famous World Game.' In 2010, Filmmaker Chris Farina released a documentary on the World Game entitled 'World Peace...and other 4th-grade achievements'. The film follows the life of 4th-grade teacher John Hunter and his utilization of the game in his classroom. Despite the challenge and the complexity of the game, the 9 and 10-year old students are able to win it and 'Achieve World Peace'. The documentary was shown at the 2011 South by Southwest Music and Film Festival and has won audience awards at various international film festivals.

## Geodesic domes

His teaching colleagues and students in the 1950's helped in the development of his most successful project, the geodesic dome, the first large scale versions of which were built at Black Mountain College.

Hailed at the time as the lightest, strongest and most cost-effective structure, the geodesic dome was designed to cover the maximum possible space without internal supports. The bigger it is, the lighter and stronger it becomes. The first full-size geodesic structure was completed – with a 49 feet diameter – in Montreal in 1950, the following year one was exhibited at the Museum of Modern Art, New York.

Dome for Expo. 67 Canada          A cardboard U-dome

**Figure 10: Two examples of Fuller domes**

In 1954 Fuller constructed two domes at the Milan Triennale exhibition made from six pieces of corrugated cardboard pre-cut in the US and folded into a small packing case for transport to Italy. Fuller's hope was that such domes could one day be manufactured at the rate of 3,000 a day.

- applying modern technological know-how to shelter construction

- making shelter more comfortable and efficient

- making shelter more economically available to a greater number of people

The U-dome from World Shelters adapts the modular geometry of Buckminster Fuller's geodesic dome. U-domes have been used for disaster response, portable medical clinics, relief agency centers, temporary housing, storage, and workshops. The patterns can easily incorporate local materials, and they are re-usable.

By 1957 Fuller had refined the design so that an enormous auditorium-sized geodesic dome was assembled in 22 hours in Honolulu. His plans for a 2 mile wide dome in Manhattan, 1960, never came to fruition but have remained the stuff of science fiction ever since.

Most domes are based on an icosahedron, which is spherical with 20 faces. It is a very strong structural shape. The 20 triangles that make up the shape can be further subdivided into smaller triangles giving eg a two-frequency icosahedron, or three frequency icosahedron. There are many varieties of dome and we will get onto that in a moment.

## Fuller's Precession Theory

'Bucky', as he is known to his fans, was incredibly creative and before his time in many ways. Ideas and inventions seemed to flow from him in a continuous stream. I would urge you to have a closer look at some of his stuff online.

But back to his 'Law of Precession' which, for me at least, is the single greatest influence from his life. From 'Critical Path':

> *"I assumed that humanity was designed to perform an important function in the Universe, a function it would discover only after an initially innocent by-trial-and-error-discovered phase of capability development.*
>
> *During the initial phase humans, always born naked, helpless and ignorant but with hunger, thirst and curiosity to drive them, have been chromosomically programmed to operate successfully only by means of the general biological inadvertencies of bumbling honey seeking [eg money making].*
>
> *Therefore what humans called the side effects of their conscious drives in fact produced the main ecological effects of generalized technological regeneration.*
>
> *I therefore assumed that what humanity rated as 'side effects' are nature's main effects. I adopted the precessional 'side effects' as my prime objective".*

Note he assumed that humanity has a purpose; we are here for a reason. This in itself is quite radical. We are not really told about this at school. Where, today do you hear people talking about a purpose for the human race? Out there, in the world of celebrity consumer capitalism, the main purpose seems to be to wreck the planet by consuming everything and turning it into rubbish to put into big holes, to watch the telly and turn expensive pre-packaged food, with its nutrition removed, into poo and cancer.

Buckminster Fuller believed that humanity has a purpose. He set out to make things that would help people to evolve, regardless sometimes of money, getting paid, having a job and all that. Most of his work was directed at helping solve problems that prevented people from being more self-sufficient. He committed not just himself but also his family, with five children to feed, to this course of action and lived, by all accounts, a very successful life in traditional terms as well as his own, at least once he started dressing more smartly and stopped being rude to people.

Let's just look at some of his observations that led to his Law of Precession idea.

When you drop a stone vertically into a lake - where do you see the effect?

**Figure 11: The precession effect takes place at a right angle to the event**

Buckminster Fuller liked bees. He observed them visiting flowers and saw that their 'intent' in being there was to collect pollen and nectar. But in doing this, the bee is quite inadvertently, cross-pollinating the flower. The 'outcome' of its actions is quite different to its 'intent'.

In a similar way the evident purpose of mankind in making war and pursuing material gain in the form of money, actually has a secondary purpose in 'evolutionary terms'. So metal created to make weapons became used to make ploughs that farm the land to create food. The Internet, designed originally for the purposes of war, has become huge interconnected networks of people leading to the democratisation of knowledge, for those people lucky enough to have access. Perhaps even contributing to the dawn of a new global consciousness.

So for me the western 'story' of: get a job, make enough money to get a mortgage, work your whole life through to get a pension, is failing dramatically. Buckminster Fuller offers us a credible replacement to that fiction and his life stands in tribute to it.

> *"The youth of today are absolutely right in recognizing this nonsense of earning a living.*
>
> *We keep inventing jobs because of this false idea that everybody has to be employed at some kind of drudgery because, according to Malthusian-Darwinian theory, he must justify his right to exist.*
>
> *The true business of people should be to go back to school and think about whatever it was they were thinking about before somebody came along and told them they had to earn a living."*

According to Fuller, start working directly for the evolution of people around you and you will find yourself mysteriously 'looked after' by those same precessional forces. Almost never in the ways you expect, always seemingly at the last minute.

Natural sciences are still catching up with the significance of his discoveries. In some cases recognition of the importance of Fuller's scientific research came only after his death. By then he had registered 25 US patents, written 28 books, traveled around the globe 57 times and received 47 honourary doctorates as well as numerous other awards including a 1969 nomination for the Nobel Peace Prize.

As someone who dislikes many of the aspects of capitalism, the sheer faith this guy had was quite stunning. I have always tried to follow his ideal and when I find myself broke, I console and motivate myself by thinking that I may not be serving the processes of evolution quite as well as I could.

I apologise if you think this section on Fuller was a distraction. To me, his domes represent not just structures – but a whole different way of looking at the subject of structure itself, which is organic in form, based on nature, interconnected and a million miles from the boxlike mentality of the Western mind and its planet killing constructs. And so… on to the domes.

# 4. An icosahedron primer

There are several ways to subdivide a sphere into a structure but the one we going to look at here is an icosahedron, a 20 faced sphere recognised even by the Ancient Greeks as one of the Platonic Solids (Tetrahedron, Cube, Octahedron, Dodecahedron, Icosahedron).

An icosahedron is a regular polyhedron with 20 identical equilateral triangular faces, 30 edges and 12 vertices. It is a form found in nature, for example some viruses have icosahedral shells.

Here is a simple method to make an icosahedron shell as a model. This is worth doing as a basic exercise for giving you a feel for this shape. Firstly, draw out 20 equilateral triangles on some thin card, in the shape shown in the picture below:

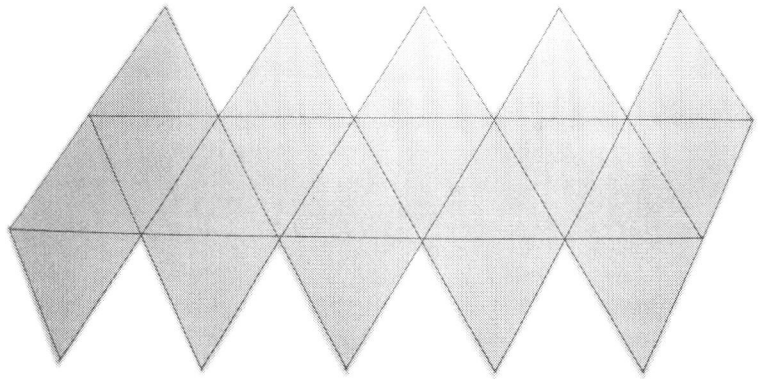

Figure 12: Layout for a cardboard icosahedron

Draw flaps around the edges of each triangle so that you can stick them together with a glue stick. Then cut out the shape and make some creases along the lines so that the icosahedron can find its shape:

Then start gluing the tab surfaces to the triangles to form a spherical shape from the cardboard. You may need to trim off some of the tabs as you go – you should end up with something like this:

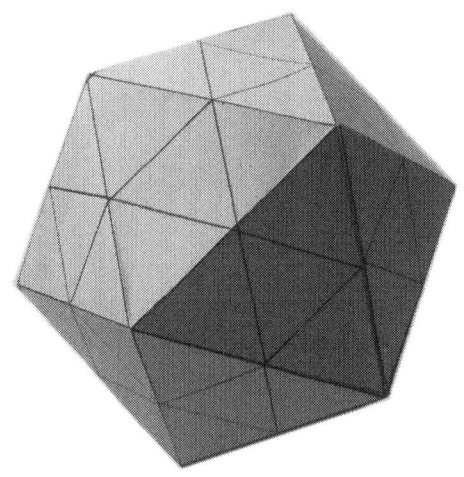

**Figure 13: Cardboard icosahedron**

I have drawn additional lines onto the shape to show how you can have different frequencies of geodesic dome, by subdividing the large equilateral triangles. If the lines were edges, this would be a two-frequency icosahedron. The smaller the triangles which go to make up the dome, the more it tends towards a sphere.

So the top five-eighths of this shape is the basic plan for my first greenhouse. As you can see from the above picture, you can 'slice' the isocahedron to make sub-shapes. It will cut at 3/8ths, a hemisphere and 5/8ths.

## Making models

Once you get on to more complicated structures with different strut lengths, it is essential to have a working model to refer to. I have found plastic drinking straws very useful for this as they come in different colours and can easily be coded using these.

The first model icosahedron above created a solid form by folding the twenty planes of the form. The next model – a three-frequency icosahedron uses drinking straws to form the struts, giving a more open and structural model.

Each one of the 20 icosahedron faces is sub-divided into nine faces (3x3) to make a three-frequency dome. The illustration below shows how this is done – giving three different strut lengths.

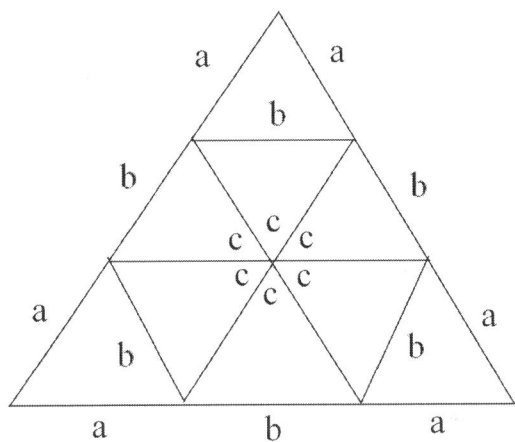

**Figure 14: Icosahedron face for a 3 frequency dome**

In a three-frequency dome there are:

- 60 struts of size a
- 90 b size struts
- 120 c size

The 'constant' chord factors for a 3 frequency are:

a = .3486

b = .4035

c = .4124

The model for this will be about 50cm in diameter (the small gaps that form in between where the struts join make it larger), a 25cm radius – so using the formula:

Chord factor x radius = length of strut

Strut a: .3486 x 25 = 8.175 cm (x 60)

Strut b: .4035 x 25 = 10.08 cm (x 90)

Strut c: .4142 x 25 = 10.35 cm (x 120)

Once you have your 270 pieces of straw cut up to size and colour coded in front of you it is time to begin the model construction.

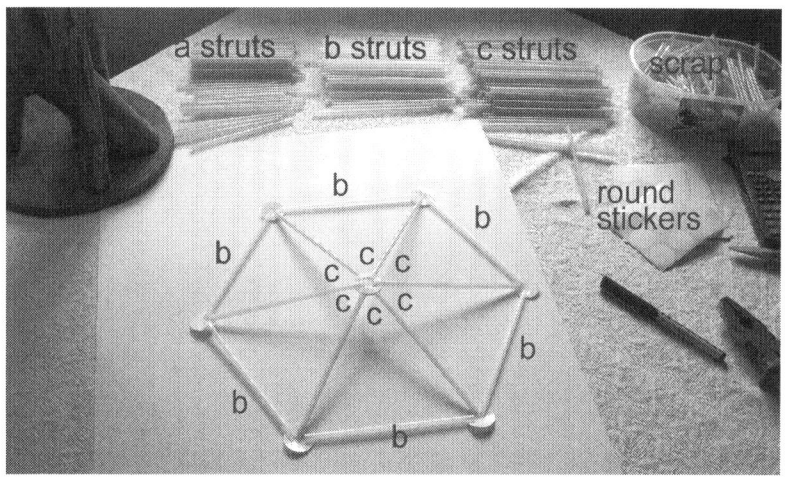

**Figure 15: First stage of model for 3 frequency dome**

I used small round stickers to hold the struts in place and once a nexus point is completed – as in the c struts above – put another sticker on facing the first. Then give the joint a gentle squeeze to stick the faces firmly together. Just a note here though, this is not a permanent solution and the model will only hold together for a certain amount of time. I made larger stickers as the model progressed, from sticky-back aluminium foil left over from lining my chimney! Some people like to melt the straws together using a hot pin – which is a bit fiddly for me – others like to use glue which I don't like as it is not long before it gets on my fingers and jams up the works!

As you might imagine, things can get quite confusing as the dome takes shape and the evening wears on. Just stick at it!

**Figure 16: Starting the evening's model dome construction**

At some stage you need to open the dome and support it to continue and complete the construction. I used a photographic tripod for this but make sure you take it out before closing the construction!

**Figure 17: The completed 3 frequency icosahedron model dome**

# 5. Icosahedron greenhouse 1

**Figure 18: Five-eighths icosahedron greenhouse**

OK, lets go full-size now with some domes of the models in previous pages. One of the attractions of this book is building a growing dome on a restricted budget, so this little piggy decided to make his icosahedron greenhouse out of fresh hazel sticks. I am lucky enough to live in the countryside with ready access to lots of hazel hedgerows.

Every day my springer spaniel, Freya, needs a walk so often when we went I out I would find and cut myself the longest-length, straight, hazel rods of a useable diameter I could find, (in addition to providing numerous sticks for the dog). Over the course of a couple of months I built my collection of sticks up to the 30 I needed.

I have just popped out to the structure to measure the length of these sticks for the first time – they are 196cm long (just over 77 inches). The reason for this seemingly arbitrary measurement is just so that I could choose the optimum length of stick available in the hedgerows – since they all needed to be the same length. I know this is building the wrong way round and if I was buying-in the struts from machined timber I would have decided on the dimensions first!

I just built the icosahedron with the optimum size of stick I could find and came out with a fair size dome with a diameter of 315cm, an internal height on the inside edges of 165cm sloping up to 230cm in the middle. To add strength and stability (and to compensate for using 'natural' materials of irregular shape) I added a central pole to the structure.

For the more scientifically orientated of you, this intuitive dome making is hardly the subject for a book. The icosahedron has 30 edges of the same length, in dome-making these are often called 'struts'. There is a relationship between the edge length and the radius. The radius of the dome is slightly less than the strut length.

With more complex domes there are multiple strut lengths. Their calculation involves a constant called a chord factor and these vary depending on what sort of dome you want to build. Some constructions, (as shown in model 2), involve several chord factors in a single dome. The chord factor involved in a basic icosahedron is 0.95. That is to say the strut length is 95% of the radius.

For a more rational building than mine in this 'country dome', firstly estimate the diameter of the icosahedron you want to build, let's say 300cm across, giving a radius of 150. To find the length of strut you need the formula is:

Chord factor x radius = length of strut

0. 95 x 150 = 142.65

So you will need 30 lengths of 142.66cm to build a 3 metre diameter dome.

It could be that to avoid the irregularities of 'wild wood' you might decide to purchase enough 2 x 1 planed timber to do the job and this is often available in packets of 10 ready cut to 200cm lengths. In this case you will need 3 packets (get 4 in case of splits). Your ready-made lengths will give you a dome of these proportions:

Chord factor x radius = length of strut

0. 951 x radius = 200 (200 divided by .951) = 210.3 x 2 = 420.6 cm diameter icosahedron.

If you estimate sawn 2x1 timber at prices at time of writing, that is 65 pence a meter 40 x 65 = 2600 = £26 (which is around $40).

The size of your dome is going to vary a bit depending on how you connect the struts to each other. There are several tried and tested methods for this, which I will demonstrate later. In an icosahedron each vertex (the singular of vertices) or node, joins five struts – a very complicated joint for joining wood to wood. So for this basic dome construction I used a simple method of drilling holes and connecting the struts with wire and rope. In order to stop the ends of my hazel from splitting, I lined each hole with a bit of used copper pipe, shown as below and let the icosahedron find its own shape.

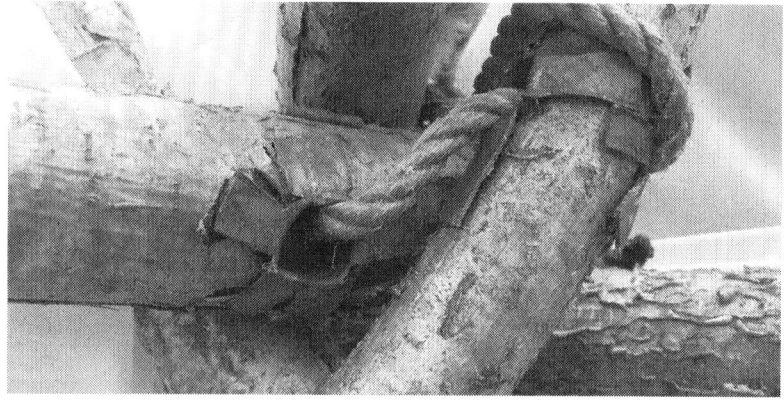

**Figure 19: Grommets made from old pipe stops the hazel splitting**

Firstly I laid out the struts in the pattern they would be constructed, six on the outside with two laid towards the centre at each joint. I had graded the struts so the least straight ones would form the base, reasonably thick hazel would form the sides of the icosahedron and the lightest, straightest hazel would form the roof struts.

**Figure 20: The struts for the sides, connected at the base**

I connected the holes on the base using fencing wire pushed through and bent over to hold the hazel secure but still allow movement. Then starting at one 'corner', I lifted the two sticks that would form a down-pointing equilateral triangle and used 2 foot lengths of high-tensile plastic rope to attach the top side of the triangle. The reason I used rope rather than wire for these is I attached three ends together, untied to add a fourth and than later, once the sides were complete, untied again to add the roof strut to each vertex. This was easier with the rope than with the fencing wire. I used reef knots to secure the vertices (right over left & under (thumb knot) then left over right and under).

This is where things got a little problematic. Once I had one side 'up' (always keeping an eye on the model) and moved onto the next, the opposite side of the 'cylinder' would collapse onto the ground and pull the structure down. One problem with geodesics is that they do not become a self-supporting structure until they are complete. I might have wished for some assistance here and muttered quietly to myself about my partner Sarah always being out, but resolved the problem by staking the poles down, like with tent poles. This allowed me to hold up the structure while it was still flimsy due to lacking the top of the icosahedron.

I then tightened-up the joints on the base to restrict their movement. I laid out the roof struts, the hazel rods tapering towards the middle, and connected them at the centre, passing the rope through all six holes of the top vertex, leaving a bit of play.

Figure 21: The dome sides up and supported with guy ropes

I moved the top to the centre of the cylinder and set it up in a tipi shape. I untied each top vertex, re-threading the rope in some instances, to attach the top struts. I supported the roof with a large stick for the last two struts. Six more reef knots and the basic structure was complete. I included a central pole to add stability to the structure, slightly lifting the roof tightened the dome up. I took another photo of my 'greenhouse' and published it on Facebook where friends and family could take the piss out of me for building a greenhouse with no glass.

**Figure 22: The icosahedron frame completed**

The covering for this dome arrived the next day. I had ordered 3 x 7.3x 1m Sunmaster Tunnel Covers, in truth without really thinking about how I was going to cover the dome. It arrived all as one big sheet. I thought I might wrap the cover around the walls of the icosahedron and then over the top but ended up cutting oversize equilateral triangle sections for each face and nailing them with small, flat-head, roofing nails onto the framework, folding over the sheeting to produce a stronger edge. This is where the fresh-cut timber came into its own – as it was still sappy it took quite a lot of pounding without splitting at all.

Three (oversized) equilateral triangles ( ΔΔ ) fitted across the width of sheet so I cut them using scissors which would 'glide' along the line drawn with maker pen. The oversize allowed for mis-shapes created by the wild wood and allowed for a fold-over onto the struts. I later tidied-up these edges by pinning them to the struts with a staple gun.

**Figure 23: The completed icosahedron greenhouse**

I alternated the first three roof sections so I could get to the struts either side with the ladder through the roof holes. It became clear when I got to the roof that I was short of sheeting but taped together right-angle triangle off-cuts to create the three roof pieces I needed. I stuck them together with aluminium foil tape left over from a chimney-lining job.

As yet I have no idea how these will stand up to the wind, I may need to replace them. The last three sections were quite hard to put up 'stretched' – they had wrinkles – I worked from the centre of the dome out to the 'wall' and put the last roof nails in from outside the dome. I also cut three plastic sheet circles (using a dustbin lid as a template) with a small central hole, and layered them between roof sheets over the central pole to stop water getting in.

I kept this greenhouse for two growing seasons and it grew tomatoes and squashes OK but had a tendency towards damp as there was not enough airflow. Some vents in the top would have allowed more air through – and also a way for the insects to get out as they had a habit of getting trapped in the ceiling area. There was also a problem with

36

keeping the grass tidy around the outside. The strimming machine would create cuts in the polytunnel lining, so it would have made more sense to raise the whole thing up slightly and let some more air underneath.

Perhaps the most dramatic event for this icosahedron is when it took off and flew across the garden during its first spring. I had meant to fix it down to the ground, but it wasn't windy and my list of 'things to do in the garden' is always long!

I didn't see it go, but I heard a great rustling in the air and went round to this part of the garden to find it had moved 25 feet, scattering tables full of seedlings across the lawn as it flew, leaving a wake like an airplane crash in its trail. Mud on top of the central pole showed that it had turned a full somersault. It was completely unharmed apart from one small rip where it had encountered a table – a tribute to the resilience of this structure.

Figure 24: The flying icosahedron greenhouse

# 6. Methods for connecting struts

People have been using geodesics for many years now and certain ways of building have become established. One of the difficulties of building geodesic domes is joining the struts as these nexus points – called a node or vertex – are often complex. They need to be rigid enough to hold the shape of the dome, yet flexible enough to cope with a bit of movement and the stresses of putting the dome together.

Here are some methods of strut joining for domes:

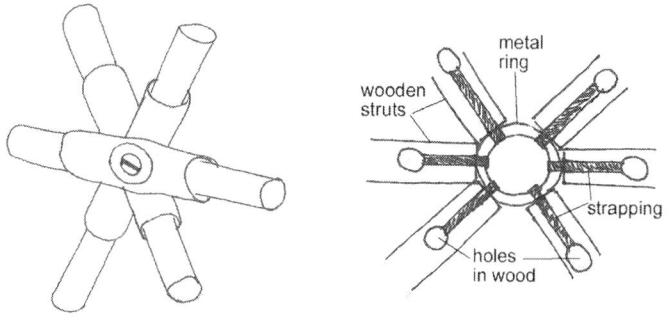

1. strut and joint       2. strapping wood to ring

**Figure 25: Strut fixing nodes**

1. The 'strut and joint' technique shown above is used in the next dome example – a three-frequency icosahedron. Its limitations became quite clear in this dome project, but it is suitable for more lightweight applications such as tents.

2. Using steel or plastic, a central ring as a hub can be strapped to a pre-drilled wooden strut. You will need to own or hire a strapping tool for this. It is not a technique I have tried as yet, as it seems quite fiddly.

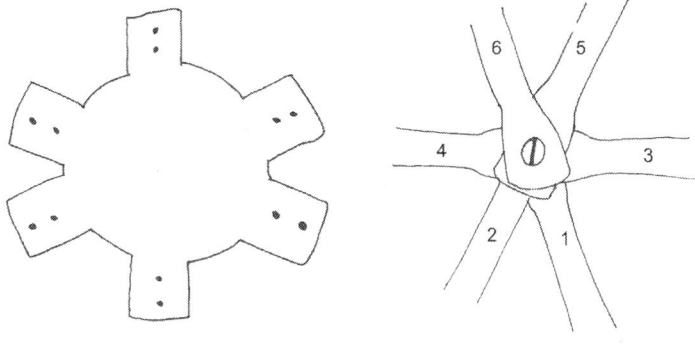

## 3. screw to a plate     4. direct jointing

**Figure 26: Strut fixing nodes 2**

3. Fixing to a plate. This is the method used in the two-frequency icosahedron growdome later in this book. It seems to work very well but you are going to get through a lot of screws. Even in a hemispherical two-frequency dome you will need more than 300 screws. I managed to find all the bits of metal I needed for this just lying around. A cardboard template made from an old box helped me pre-drill all the holes in the right places.

4. Direct jointing: One of the simplest solutions I have seen. Particularly good for larger domes made from scaffolding poles. The end of the poles are flattened and angled suitably and a hole drilled through them to take a bolt and washers. It is important to put these struts together in the right order to balance the stresses in the dome. The domes I saw using this technique are regularly moved during the summer for festivals – a simple but strong solution.

# 7. Three Frequency Icosahedron

This is my second greenhouse icosahedron and it suffers from over-complexity. A three-frequency dome was one two many frequencies for its size. It took quite some time to manufacture and build although it actually cost next to nothing in materials.

The materials for this one were bamboo and old hosepipe for the rigid structure, and recycled plastic sheeting for the cover. I started off with the model shown earlier for making a three-frequency dome.

**Figure 27: Model dome for the three-frequency icosahedron**

Next I spent an evening cutting all the old, leaky hosepipe I could find into about six inch lengths, until I had a generous bucketful – there's a proper country measurement for you ! OK, that's 240 lengths of six inch hosepipe in order to make 80 x 6 joint connectors as shown in the next illustration.

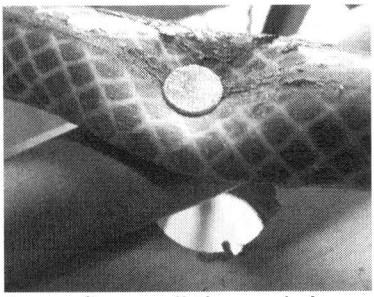
1. roofing nail through hose

2. compress hoses

3. mole grips to hold head

4. hammer nail over

**Figure 28: making the joint connectors**

I had decided on a 3 metre wide 5/8 dome – giving a radius of 150 cm, but decided to make enough struts for a whole sphere. This gave me a strut length calculation as follows (see fig.14 for illustration):

a – chord factor .3486 x 150 = 52.3cm x 60 struts

b – chord factor .4035 x 150 = 60.5cm x 90 struts

c – chord factor .4124 x 150 = 61.9cm x 90 struts

I added the strut length for a,b and c together which came to 176 cm and my bamboo came in 183cm (6 foot) lengths. So I estimated I should get 120 six-foot lengths of bamboo from the garden centre because I am not very good at maths and bamboo is really useful in the garden. This worked out at time of making as 11 pence per stick – a total of £13.20 on bamboo.

I took the bus to 'Trago Mills' which runs on the first Tuesday of every month a couple of miles from where I live, and bought them there. All the old ladies on the bus on the way back kept trying to engage me in conversations about growing peas and runner beans. Walking home from St. Breward with 120 bamboo sticks was a bit of an ordeal but nothing compared to what was to come.

1.saw bench with strut sizes

2.sawn to length & marked

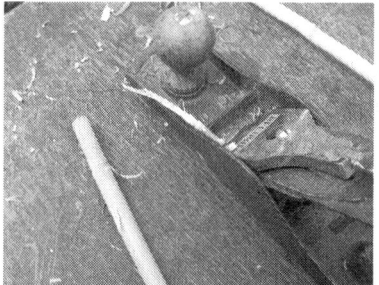
3. rough ends chamfered

4. struts stacked & ready

Figure 29: sawing up the bamboo to strut lengths

The hacksaw seemed best on the bamboo and I set-up my production factory for struts, marking out the three different lengths on a bench with masking tape. I colour-coded the different strut lengths with electrical insulation tape I had purchased on my trip to Trago. Many of the bamboo struts seem to end on a knobbly bit so I chamfered them down with a wood plane and stacked them in separate buckets for the next stage – the build.

Even with a model and hand and all of the struts carefully colour-coded, this was a nightmare. I had started off by pre-making all of the 'c' strut nodes and got so far before the structure would just turn to chaos before my eyes. It wouldn't stand up, everything flopped around all over the place. I gave up several times.

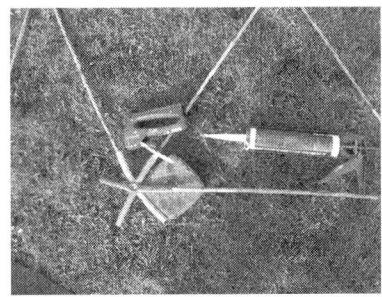

1. pre-made 'c' nodes    2. staples and acrylic filler

3. the first stage went well    4. but soon, floppy chaos

**Figure 30: putting the dome framework together was a nightmare**

One of the problems was that the bamboo had different diameters so it didn't all fit neatly into the hose joints. A squirt of acrylic filler and some staples through the hose into the bamboo helped fix this, but it meant that every joint had to be assembled on the ground, to get the opposing pressure for the stapler to work. After a stage this was impossible.

I held the dome structure up with bits of wood, string, garden furniture, gardening tools, trees, shrubs and prayer and eventually it started to take shape as something vaguely ovoid. It took many hours and bamboo haunted my dreams for nights.

Although I had put it together in a conveniently open part of the garden, it was not where I intended to site the dome, so I had to take it apart in sections and move it to the site for re-assembly.

I'm skimming over this part a bit as I don't want the nightmares of a seemingly endless, impossible and futile task to start again. Bit by bit, it appeared in the right place and I covered it with recycled polythene, some from a canoe we had delivered, bubblewrap from packaging, old dog food bags (at the base) and bits of random polythene packaging. I left some gaps in the top of the dome so it could breathe.

Finally, in late spring, simon gives birth to a giant egg

Figure 31: the dome installed in position

The framework didn't survive the transplant too well and by the time I had stapled layers of recycled polythene all over it, was starting to sag. I wrapped the base in cling film a few times to add a bit of squeeze to the structure.

The dome actually grew stuff quite well but I think that this was partly due to the fact that I had put it (and tied it down to) a base of concrete made from some old garage walls. I had my best ever Basil crop. The concrete base created a terrific heat sink that would keep the dome warm late into the evening. That year – I grew my first melon, albeit a bit too late to ripen.

Inside the egg dome       my first melon appears

Figure 32: inside the dome

In the second year, I decided to shore the roof up a bit with a vertical column of strawberry pots, which cropped so well that the blackbirds came in to get them through the holes in the roof until I stopped them with netting.

the strawberry tower before and after cropping

Figure 33: the strawberry tower

# 8. Two frequency Icosahedron

Given the benefit of some experience with my two domes I felt it was time to invest a bit of money and make one with some 'proper wood'. This one was to be a five-eighths, two frequency icosahedron, raised-up from the ground on a sort of plinth.

By this time I had found the dome calculation software at www.desertdomes.com, which made working out strut lengths and amounts a much easier calculation. The page gave me the following calculation for a 6.5 foot radius dome:

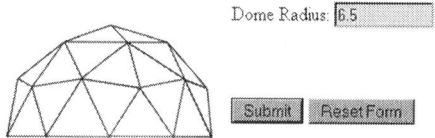

Don't include units here. For example, if you want to build a dome that's 10' 6" high, enter 10.5

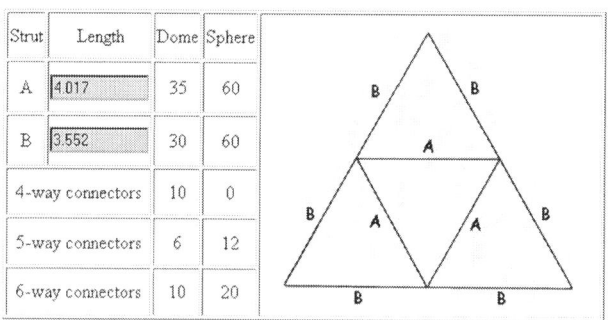

| Strut | Length | Dome | Sphere |
|-------|--------|------|--------|
| A | 4.017 | 35 | 60 |
| B | 3.552 | 30 | 60 |
| 4-way connectors | | 10 | 0 |
| 5-way connectors | | 6 | 12 |
| 6-way connectors | | 10 | 20 |

**Figure 34: 2V calculation page from desertdomes.com**

It also made the calculations for another straw model much easier and thankfully this dome was a lot more straightforward than the three frequency. I ordered 30 x 4.8 metre lengths of treated timber and before long my straw model and 65, A and B struts were cut, colour coded and awaiting my attention. I had decided to cut enough strut lengths for a hemisphere and see how it went from there.

**Figure 35: A and B strut lengths with full sphere model**

I experimented with connectors for this dome. I wanted something that was clean, simple and strong and that justified an investment of around £70 worth of treated timber. Plastic downpipe for guttering seemed like a flexible, yet strong option and I made up some joints riveting and screwing struts into these, then strengthening the joint with a larger pipe. It was all too complicated and making 26 of these would be much too time consuming.

In the end I opted for the much simpler solution of cutting out metal discs using hand shears and pre-drilling them using cardboard templates. The dome required a mixture of five and six strut connectors – also some special ones, which connect the bottom of the hemisphere to the anchor points in the ground. And when I say pre-drilling I mean putting the cardboard template over the zinc sheet and making holes through it with a great big nail and hammer.

1. rivets, metal, plastic pipe   2. screw through pipe

3. rivet angle iron            4. pipe joint strengthener

Figure 36: Experiments with strut joints

 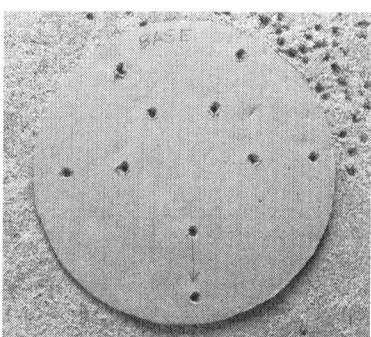

5 and 6 strut templates        base template

Figure 37: cardboard templates to locate screw holes

starting with the apex          the dome takes shape

Figure 38: stacking tyres under the dome as it grows

the top connections needed additional support

Figure 39: bolts through wooden discs to reinforce the top 6 joints

a perfect hemisphere arises from the mud

Figure 40: the completed hemispherical framework

With an electric screwdriver was quite easy to connect the struts to the node connectors with screws. There were a few splits where the wood was weak but it was simple to drill the occasional additional hole. There was a lot of movement in the top section (fig. 38) so this required some reinforcement in the form of stout bolts through the middle of the struts, with some discs of scrap wood either side to create enough pressure to stabilise the joint.

The tyres needed quite a bit of shifting around to build the dome up as it took shape, allowing room underneath for the next strut. A few hour's work and the basic hemisphere was built. Although I had intended a 5/8 dome, it was immediately apparent that, once the hemisphere was raised a touch, there would easily be enough room for a good size greenhouse.

The next stage then, taking my first wind-blown dome into consideration, was to anchor this one properly to the ground. I dug holes underneath each base node point and put in uprights, concreted in. This technique allowed me to level the structure at the base as I went around, using a spirit level along each lateral strut.

Figure 41: base struts leveled and connected to concreted uprights

slate shuttering and cement    brick and block work

**Figure 42: filling the gaps under the dome**

There were several techniques used to fill the gaps under the dome, based mainly on what materials I had to hand. Two of the gaps I filled with engineering bricks I had sitting around. These have holes through them, which allows for a good air flow into the dome. Another two I used blocks and bricks.

Two sides I shuttered with slates and in-filled with a mix of recycled dog food tins and cement. If necessary I can puncture through the tins to increase air-flow. I expect they will rust away after a couple of years anyway.

Another two sides I simply cut some leftover carpet to size and stapled it to the base struts, adding some slates as well. Before long my base was reasonably sealed-in and awaiting a floor.

**Figure 43: gaps under the base filled-in using several methods**

**Figure 44: the door construction and top window placement**

For an entrance I took out a cross-strut and bent some fresh hazel into shape to replace the lost force. I tied the hazel into the struts either side and nailed through the hazel into the adjacent vertical struts.

For the window I made an inner frame for one of the top triangles and stretched and old umbrella cover over it to add a bit of colour! I also put polytunnel cover over this for waterproofing. It leaks a little bit but that doesn't matter – in fact I sometimes put an under-watered pot under where the drips land. The window opens and closes using a hinge made from the rubber of old Wellington boots, one of my favourite 'Cornish hinges'. Having an open space in the roof is not just essential for cooling on hot days, it also allowed me to get at the roof to staple the cover on.

I dug a drain in the centre of the dome, which runs to one side where there is a septic tank nearby. I am considering putting in a solar-heated shower at some point for use on summer days.

**Figure 45: Laying the crazy paving base**

The dome that had been in this position previously (the three-frequency 'egg') had one really good quality, the concrete base on which it stood worked extremely well as a passive heat store, so I wanted to recreate this by laying a base of rocks.

I had been saving black, plastic, dog food bags from dry food for this very purpose but didn't have quite enough. The base of this dome is rife with bindweed and I didn't want it creeping in and climbing over everything, so the plastic sheet was to seal out light and seal in creeping bindweed. I had some bits of granite, slate, local flat rocks and proceeded to make a rock jigsaw of the base. This took a lot longer than I expected but by the time the sand and cement arrived, I had enough rocks and a basic idea of where to put them.

I would mix up cement and lay a square yard or so a day for quite a while, until, finally I had a base for my dome. I put some of the more mis-shaped rocks around the outside and painted them black to increase their capacity to absorb the heat from sunlight during the day.

**Figure 46: floor complete, workbench installed and the start of the cover**

I ordered another £30 worth of polytunnel cover as I was also going to recycle the cover from my first dome by re-cutting the triangles. I built a detachable window in the side (bottom left of fig.46) so that I could easily lift pots, soil, harvests etc in and out of the dome. I also used the leftover wood (I had ordered enough for a 5/8 dome) to construct a bench inside the dome.

Starting with the base triangles, I cut, stapled and trimmed each triangle individually. The next level up, this meant that water would run down over the triangles underneath, rather than into the dome. Again, this took quite some time and by the time I was up on the top run with a ladder, I was getting quite gymnastic as well. I also sealed every single joint with special waterproof tape made for polytunnel plastic. The entrance needed a 'porch' to protect it from downpours but it was not difficult to bend a bit more fresh hazel to the task and cover this with the sheeting.

Figure 47: inside the completed growdome

Figure 48: the two-frequency growdome

Printed by Amazon Italia Logistica S.r.l.
Torrazza Piemonte (TO), Italy